The Intimate Marriage

DAVID & CAROLE HOCKING

HARVEST HOUSE PUBLISHERS
Eugene, Oregon 97402

THE INTIMATE MARRIAGE

Taken from **ROMANTIC LOVERS**
Copyright © 1986 by David and Carole Hocking
Published by Harvest House Publishers
Eugene, Oregon 97402

ISBN 0-89081-696-4

The Beauty of Romance

Romance! What a beautiful word! It belongs in every marriage, but so few couples seem to experience it. We feel it at first . . . uncontrollable sensations, often caused by just a glance or a smile . . . strong during courtship as we're filled with anticipation in looking forward to that special wedding day!

Why is it that so many couples stop being romantic after the marriage takes place? Why do we spend so little time adoring, admiring, and appreciating each other? Why is it easier to compliment someone other than our marital partner?

After years of marital struggle and what we call "quiet tension," we decided to change. It didn't happen overnight; it took time. But it was well worth the effort. And the best help for romantic love within a marriage is found in the Song of Solomon. This is romance par excellence!

Solomon gives God's viewpoint, and that's vitally important. The secular world speaks much of romantic love but offers very few guidelines for true love. Morals and ethics are usually left out. Solomon tells you how "falling in love" should happen when God's love controls you and when His principles determine your feelings.

1

The Song of Songs

Song of Solomon 1:1-4

The song of songs, which is Solomon's. What an opening line to the most powerful romantic story ever written! It tells us several things. It speaks of music; it is a song—not just an ordinary song, but *The* Song of Songs! Romantic love done in God's way is filled with music—the music of love!

Musical songs are poetic, and the Song of Solomon is saturated with romantic poetry and beautiful vocabulary. It tells us how couples who are in love communicate with each other. There is nothing here of crass, blunt, sarcastic, or critical talk. It is sweet and refreshing to the heart.

Mary and Henry had been married for six years, but now things were going sour. Critical words passed between them on a daily basis, and neither one of them was happy with the results. Both wanted to change but didn't know where to begin. It's hard to admit we're wrong and start over!

When I asked them about their communication with each other, I knew I was on the right track. They both admitted that it was not good. Some of their difficulty began with the kind of communication they shared while making love. They had not been Christians for very long, and the words they used with each other came from the streets, not from the heart of God. I shared some of the verses from Solomon's Song with them, and they both started laughing. I admit that it does seem a little strange at first. After some explanation and a few more passages, they started to settle down and pay attention to the romance of this book.

This story has a happy ending. Mary and Henry decided to read the Song of Solomon repeatedly and to begin to communicate with each other along the lines of this beautiful love song. In a few weeks their relationship was radically changed, and today they are very happy.

Sexual communication today has become ugly. Sexual aggressiveness and violent intentions have been promoted by our culture, and obscenity is often expressed by couples in the secrecy of the bedroom. How tragic!

But it doesn't have to be that way. It is so much more rewarding and healthy for a couple to speak romantically as Solomon and Abishag did in this beautiful love song. The words we use today may be more contemporary than those used 3000 years ago, but they should be the best and most beautiful of all that we know and have.

How to Know
If You Have Fallen in Love

Let him kiss me with the kisses of his mouth—for your love is better than wine. Because of the fragrance of your good ointments, your name is ointment poured forth; therefore the virgins love you. Lead me away! We will run after you. The king has brought me into his chambers. We will be glad and rejoice in you. We will remember your love more than wine.

These verses present three ways in which we can know if we have fallen in love. They speak from the wife's point of view.

1. When his caresses (lovemaking) are more desirable than any celebration (1:2).
2. When his character is more desirable than his cologne (1:3).
3. When his companionship is more desirable than the company of all other people (1:4).

About Those Caresses

Abishag spoke of Solomon's lovemaking as being better than wine, the symbol of enjoyment and celebration. This wife sees her husband's sexual responses to her as better than any human celebration on earth!

Many Christian couples are not sure what the Bible says about sexual pleasure. We are all aware of how much enjoyment we can receive while engaged in it, but some of us are not sure if it is carnal or spiritual. Hebrews 13:4 should clarify this point for all of us: *"Marriage is honorable among all, and the bed undefiled."*

Ann saw one of our women counselors about the problems that she and Jack were having. She briefly told me that she was not being fulfilled by Jack's lovemaking skills, and wondered if we had anyone who could help her. One of our ladies listened to her story, and then told me I ought to see Jack. It seems that he reacted adversely to sex for pleasure, believing that it was only a necessary duty in order to propagate the human race!

The day we talked is still fresh in my mind. It was unusual in one sense: Most men do not have this problem. Jack had been raised in a very strict and religious home. He has been taught this view of sex since he was a child, and he firmly believed it. When I inquired about whether he had any desire to give or receive pleasure through sexual involvement with his wife, he said that he did but that he always tried to confess it immediately to God and suppress it in his mind and heart.

Frankly, I was delighted to deal with a person like Jack. He really loved the Lord and was greatly loved by his wife, Ann. They needed a biblical answer. When I showed him Hebrews 13:4, he was amazed. When we read a few of the passages in the Song of Solomon, he seemed embarrassed. I asked him what he thought. I've always appreciated his answer: "It's none of your business, but I think I would like to talk to my wife about it." We both agreed, and had prayer together.

A few weeks later I spotted them in church, and by the smile on his wife's face I knew that things had improved. After the service he said to me, "Pastor, I'm finding it hard these days to leave the house for work!"

Are you still excited about the caresses of your spouse? People in love can't wait to touch each other again.

How Does He Smell?

The second evidence that you are in love is when his character is more desirable than his cologne!

Because of the fragrance of your good ointments, your name is ointment poured forth.

Carole and I both use perfumes, but the perfumes we use are not worthy to be compared with the smell of the heart. What we are really like in our hearts is much more important than our outward appearance or smell. Couples in love are attracted by the personality of the spouse. Ecclesiastes 7:1 says, "A good name [character] is better than precious ointment." How true!

Alone at Last

When you are in love, you treasure the moments alone. You can't wait to be together, away from all other people. The third characteristic of lovers focuses on intimate companionship. When his companionship is more desirable than the company of all others, you are in love!

Couples who have no time to be alone with each other are making a big mistake. It affects the quality of their marriage whether they want to admit it or not. Every couple needs to plan time together alone. After the children are born, the pressures and struggles for privacy are increased. But the need remains, and sometimes even gets stronger. If not fulfilled by your spouse, the need is often fulfilled by someone else, and more serious difficulties arise that often lead to divorce.

2

The Need for Apples and Cakes of Raisins

Song of Solomon 2:4-6

Does food turn you on? Some people feel sexual desire by looking at certain foods (especially fruits), and others get excited by eating! Sometimes a certain food is associated with a pleasant sexual experience. Perhaps you and your spouse enjoy eating in bed, and what you eat together or feed each other makes you think warm thoughts toward your partner.

Carole and I enjoy frozen yogurt. Solomon and Abishag were into apples and raisin cakes. So was the entire ancient world, for these were erotic symbols and reminded people of sexual desire. The sweetness of those items was no doubt the reason for the association.

The Desire to Make Love

Verses 4-6 in chapter 2 contain a brief summary of their wedding-night experience which

11

will be discussed in more detail in the following chapter. It is approached from the wife's point of view. Abishag has been drawn romantically to Solomon and is now expressing her desire to make love to him.

The majority of husbands get really excited when they know that their wives are romantically aroused by them and truly desire to make love. When the wife never wants such sexual experience, it is a real turnoff to the husband.

Alex talked one day about his growing disappointment with Betty. He loved her, but was never really sure that she wanted him. He did not seem to doubt her love for him, but he spoke of it in rather platonic terms. He frankly asked if it was wrong for a husband to expect his wife to want sex. Alex's question is one which many husbands have experienced. There are times and temperaments which do not seem to require great sexual interest and arousal on the part of husbands and wives. A little understanding and patience goes a long way.

After further conversation with both Alex and Betty, it was obvious that Alex's attitudes were deeply affecting his wife, though he was unaware of them. When Alex changed the way he spoke and acted, Betty changed.

We couldn't help but compare Alex's problem with the romantic attitudes and kindness of King Solomon. No wonder Abishag was attracted to this man! He loved her and spoke with appreciation for her appearance and character. His compliments drew her to him.

But the other side of the story is reflected often. It is possible for wives to miss the need of their husbands for their sexual love and aggressiveness. Husbands need to be desired by their wives just as wives need their husbands to desire them. It is not wrong for the wife to desire sex with her husband. She is not simply a tool for him to use to satisfy his needs, but she has a right to sexual enjoyment and satisfaction as well. The truth is that the husband needs to know that his wife desires to make love with him!

Sustain me with cakes of raisins, refresh me with apples, for I am lovesick.

Abishag is in love! Her passion is now taking over. She can hardly wait to feel his touch and to experience the joy of his sexual love for her.

The raisin and the apple, because of their sweetness, suggest that this lovesick girl can only be rescued from her sexual passion by the embraces and kisses of her lover. When a wife experiences this kind of passion, the husband is indeed rewarded!

Abishag uses the words "sustain me" and "refresh me." It sounds selfish, but within the context of marital love it is perfectly legitimate for the wife to experience such powerful desire. The question is, will the husband be able to sustain and refresh such a wife? Many men are too selfish in their sexual lovemaking to allow this kind of scene to develop. Husbands need to be patient and loving toward their wives. Women are not aroused as quickly as men, but when they do experience such passion, it is a wonderful thing for the husband to behold. He will be rewarded if he is patient, loving and kind toward her needs. After all, according to Ephesians 5:25-33, husbands are to reflect the love of Jesus Christ toward their wives. It means that they must be willing to sacrifice personal desires and needs in order to please and satisfy their wives.

3

Let's Get Married!

Song of Solomon 3:6-11

What beautiful occasions weddings are! What a moment it is when the organist or pianist plays that wedding march and the bride, with her arm on her father's, begins her procession down the aisle. It's a time to celebrate!

Where Does the Wedding Take Place?

Who is this coming out of the wilderness like pillars of smoke?

The word "wilderness" is used 270 times in the Old Testament and refers to pastureland. This is a reference to the bride's home. The engagement usually took place in the bride-groom's home, and the wedding procession (usually a year later) started at the bride's home and ended at the couple's new residence.

The words "Who is this?" are feminine. They refer to Abishag, the bride, or possibly to Solomon's couch mentioned in 3:7 (feminine noun). In 6:10 such an expression is applied to Abishag, so it would seem natural and logical to take these words as referring to Abishag as she sits upon a special wedding couch which Solomon has prepared for her.

The words "coming out of the wilderness" speak of contrast as Solomon sees her coming. She is obviously a gorgeous sight, and it seems quite amazing that she comes out of country life rather than from the beautiful surroundings of the palace.

How Come She Smells So Good?

Perfumed with myrrh and frankincense, with all the merchant's fragrant powders.

Abishag did not have these exotic fragrances available in her country surroundings. They were provided by Solomon, and were indications of his great love for her. He provided her with all the perfumes any woman could ever hope to use, and saw to it that she was marvelously prepared for this very special day.

In 1:11 Solomon promised to adorn her. Now in 3:6, we see how he fulfills that promise. No doubt he sent a caravan of people and supplies to prepare his beautiful bride for the wedding procession.

God's love is being pictured here. Solomon is like our Lord, though even with his wealth and great example he comes far short of our Savior's loving care for us. We smell good because He has made us beautiful, covering us with the fragrances of His love for us. He is the loving, caring Bridegroom, and we are the bride. The day of our wedding celebration has not yet arrived, but we wear the engagement ring of His salvation and rest in the security of His promises to us.

What About Solomon's Couch?

It may sound strange to twentieth-century ears, but Solomon wanted his bride to be carried. He did not want her feet to be hurt and worn out by the long journey. He prepared a couch upon which she should be carried. This would immediately show to everyone how much he loved her and honored her.

One of the great needs of our day is for husbands to honor their wives. First Peter 3:7 contains these important words: *"Likewise you husbands, dwell with them with understanding, giving honor to the wife, as to the weaker vessel, and as being heirs together of the grace of life, that your prayers may not be hindered."*

The Bible teaches that husbands are to give honor to their wives, and that failure to do so results in unanswered prayers.

Harry and Rebecca had lots of struggles in their 12 years of marriage. She resisted him continually, and he did not seem to enjoy her presence or her communication. He was always criticizing her in public and revealing her "many faults" to others. One day he shared with us his frustration, and said, "Frankly, I don't like the woman!"

We were not the only ones who suspected that he felt this way. It was obvious by his attitudes toward his wife and the things he said about her. We confronted him with 1 Peter 3:7 about honoring his wife, and he laughed. He said that it would be impossible for him to honor his wife until she "shaped up."

When he heard us encourage him to honor his wife because God commanded him to do so, he became nervous and defensive. He responded, "If I did that, she would get a big head!" Presumably this meant that she could not handle such honor and would become unbearably proud and conceited by all the honor he might bestow! This frankly amused us, since he had shown no respect for her in the past.

The good news is that Harry started to respond to what the Bible teaches. It was difficult for him at first. There were so many things he wanted to change in Rebecca's life. Interestingly, when he stopped trying to change her, and began to honor her for the woman she was and for the good things that she did, she started to change. Today he is thrilled with the results, and they seem to have a brand-new start in their married life together.

Here Comes the Bridegroom!

Song of Solomon 3:9,10 pictures the bridegroom in all his glory:

Of the wood of Lebanon Solomon the king made himself a palanquin: He made its pillars of silver, its support of gold, its seat of purple, its interior paved with love by the daughters of Jerusalem.

A "palanquin" is a seat or (in this case) a throne. Solomon's throne was unique in that the finest wood in the world was used—the wood of Lebanon. The strength of this unique seat was found in its "pillars of silver," which portrays a person of great wealth. The "gold" and "purple" are materials speaking of royalty and majesty, fitting for this bridegroom, the king of Israel!

The most fascinating part of Solomon's throne is its carvings or pavings. Song of Solomon 3:10 says that its interior was "paved with love by the daughters of Jerusalem." When these courtly ladies and bridal attendants thought about the character of Solomon, they responded by carving love symbols into his throne. According to what we learn from ancient customs, this throne was probably paved, lined, or carved with scenes of lovemaking. In it we see Solomon as the great lover, emphasizing the role of the husband in the love relationship.

What the Wedding Means to the Bridegroom

Song of Solomon 3:11 emphasizes what this wedding celebration meant to Solomon:

Go forth, O daughters of Zion, and see King Solomon with the crown with which his mother crowned him on the day of his espousals, the day of the gladness of his heart.

The Bible says that this wedding day which brought together Solomon and Abishag was "the day of the gladness of his heart." What a wonderful conclusion to this marvelous wedding procession and celebration! As Solomon wrote these words later, how sweet to see that his marriage to Abishag was a day that brought great joy to his heart!

Solomon wrote in Ecclesiastes 9:9: *Live joyfully with the wife whom you love all the days of your vain life which He has given you under the sun, all your days of vanity; for that is your portion in life, and in the labor which you perform under the sun."*

Many marriages would be different if husbands realized this principle and applied it: A wife is a great blessing and should fill your heart and life with joy. God wants our marriage to bring us much happiness.

Does the day of your marriage bring joy and gladness to your heart, or do you wish that you had never been married? Is your wife filling your mind and heart with joy, or do you wish you had married someone else?

How Would You Evaluate Your Marriage?

Every now and then we need to take a deep breath and take time to evaluate our marriage. Do we still have that original joy? Are we still excited about making love together? Do thoughts of our partners cause us to be thankful and to rejoice in God's institution of marriage? If not, why not? What has gone wrong? How can we get the joy back?

Starting with Song of Solomon chapter 4, this beautiful love poem is going to give intimate details about how a husband and a wife should respond to each other if they would "live joyfully" together.

A strong feature for this love song is that of sexual desire and relationship. Since this is the Word of God, we cannot help but conclude that sexual matters play a crucial role in a good marriage. When a couple speaks disparagingly about sex within marriage, trouble is not far around the corner.

Sex was invented by God for the propagation of the human race—no doubt about that But it was also intended by God to bring pleasure to husband and wife. Unfortunately, many couples still struggle with this truth. The Song of Solomon makes it abundantly clear that God wants us to enjoy each other within the boundaries of His institution of marriage.

4

You Have Ravished My Heart

Song of Solomon 4:1–5:1

The wedding night has arrived; the ceremony is over; the couple is alone. What a privilege to be spectators! Under normal conditions the bedroom is private, but God allows us to view this sexual experience for our understanding. He wants to make sure we know what to do and how to do it.

Many specific sexual techniques are missing in this love poem. You can read about them in scores of books designed to help couples adjust to each other's sexual needs and difficulties. In our opinion, the Song of Solomon is all you need. The principles and insights of sexual love-making presented in this book can produce a wonderful marriage relationship and bring complete sexual satisfaction. The tragedy is that so few people give it much credit. They do not explore the meaning of these romantic and poetic words or apply the kind of love which exists between Solomon and Abishag.

Two things are dealt with in the first 11 verses of chapter 4, the wedding night of Solomon and Abishag:

1. Solomon's DESCRIPTION of his wife's beauty (4:1-7).
2. Solomon's DESIRE for his wife's affection (4:8-11).

Solomon does all the talking here, suggesting that the responsibility of lovemaking rests primarily upon the husband. The wife needs reassurance that this man who dated her and spoke so romantically to her during those days is really the tender and loving husband that she expects him to be. The beginning moments of a couple's life together should be handled carefully and prayerfully. Husbands need patience, tenderness, gentleness, and loving concern for their wives, not just on the wedding night but all through the marriage.

The Pleasures of Love

Solomon, having expressed his love verbally, is now ready to express it physically. This is the climax of their desire for each other, the celebration of their wedding night!

1. *Sexual pleasure is based on the attraction of the husband to his wife.*

Solomon pictures the sexual delights of his wife, Abishag, as though she were a "garden."

Similar word pictures are found in the writings of ancient cultures in love poetry. Plants, fruits, and fragrances were all used as erotic symbols, picturing the sexual relationship and pleasures of marriage.

He was attracted by her fidelity.

A garden enclosed is my sister, my spouse,
a spring shut up, a fountain sealed.

The emphasis here is on the fact that she is a virgin. She has protected her sexual fruits and delicious waters from others and saved them for the one she would marry. Solomon is deeply attracted to this commitment.

Abishag's sexuality is described as a "garden," a "spring," and a "fountain." Solomon found her "enclosed," "shut up," and "sealed." Obviously from 4:16, Abishag has now removed the locks and barriers and invited Solomon to enjoy himself.

He was attracted by her fruits.

Your plants are an orchard
of pomegranates with pleasant fruits.

The words "plants" is referring to her sexuality. Solomon saw her as an "orchard of pomegranates" and not just as one tree or one plant. There were many facets to her sexual desires and delights. Her "fruits" were "pleasant," a delight to his heart. These symbols of love are all intended to emphasize the pleasure which can be experienced within the marriage relationship.

The words "fruits" indicated the joy of tasting and eating. The erotic overtones of this romantic passage are quite obvious, and commentators who try to avoid it or allegorize these words are missing the point. A worse consequence is when allegorical interpretations lead us to believe that sexual pleasure is not the intention of God for marriage.

He was attracted by her fragrances.

> *Fragrant henna with spikenard,*
> *spikenard and saffron, calamus and cinnamon,*
> *with all trees of frankincense, myrrh and aloes,*
> *with all the chief spices.*

It is possible that these smells were the result of Abishag being bathed in exotic perfumes, which were readily available and were collected by King Solomon from all over the world. However, the point of this passage is that Abishag herself causes these smells. There are her "plants" and her "spices." Solomon is speaking of her sexuality and how wonderful is her smell in the midst of lovemaking. How sweet of Solomon to speak of this to his bride and to assure her that he continued to be attracted by all that she brings forth!

He was attracted by her fountain.

> *A fountain of gardens, a well of*
> *living waters, and streams from Lebanon.*

What beautiful and romantic language! Her sexual response to him was like "living waters" and the delicious-tasting "streams of Lebanon" that come down the slopes of Mount Hermon. How wonderfully refreshing they are! Solomon pictures his bride that way. Her sexuality is like the most delicious-tasting water—nothing can compare with it.

It is possible (though not conclusive) that Solomon is referring to the sexual release of his bride in these beautiful phrases. If so, then we must say that no book written by human ingenuity could possibly improve on or add anything more to our sexual understanding. This is God's Word, and though our human interpretation is fallible and often misses the mark of what God intended, we believe that everything written in this beautiful Song of Songs is infallible and the very best instruction that any married couple could possibly obtain.

2. *Sexual pleasure is based on the attitude of the wife toward her husband's desire.*

A Christian wife was struggling with the sexual desires and passion she saw in her husband. He was a good man and loved the Lord, but he was hurting from her reluctance. We tried to talk to them about God's love, but we sensed that there was more to her story than we were hearing.

Carole was able to identify with her, and helped her to relax and share what was bothering her. It seems that her mother had planted the thought in her head that men were animals, and that their sexual desires were nothing but carnal passion, unrelated to true spiritual love. It was something to be endured, not enjoyed. Men were to be pitied for "their problem." She seemed surprised when Carole shared the Bible's view of sexual desire and pleasure.

After several occasions in which these issues were discussed with a Christian female counselor, this wife began to see her problem. She was able to confess to her husband and ask for his forgiveness. She literally set him free, and their marriage started to grow once more. The interesting thing was how much his public ministry changed. He had a new joy and freedom in sharing God's Word with other people, and definitely seemed more relaxed and contented.

Awake, O north wind, and come, O south!
Blow upon my garden, that its spices
may flow out. Let my beloved come to his
garden and eat its pleasant fruits.

In Song of Solomon 2:7 and 3:5 she had previously said, "Do not awaken love." Now she says, "Awake!" The prohibition was necessary before marriage; after the wedding no such restriction is applied.

3. *Sexual pleasure is based on the acceptance of sexual satisfaction and unity by both husband and wife.*

I have come to my garden, my sister, my spouse;
I have gathered my myrrh with my spice;

I have eaten my honeycomb with my honey;
I have drunk my wine with my milk.

Both partners must agree with what takes place when they make love with each other. Sexual pleasure depends on such mutual acceptance by both partners. When one partner disagrees with what is desired or practiced, it will be difficult for sexual pleasure to be experienced and enjoyed as it should be.

Notice how this verse blends things together:

"my myrrh with my spice"
"my honeycomb with my honey"
"my wine with my milk"

These combinations reveal that both partners are enjoying their sexual relationship and are finding it as satisfying as they had desired when they started. That's the way it should be in any marriage ruled by God's Word and controlled by His love.

Often we are asked about the morality and validity of certain sexual acts and practices within marriage. From a technical side, everything within marriage is acceptable, while anything outside of marriage is denied.

But more needs to be said. When one partner demands a certain sexual activity from the other partner, it is unlikely that it will produce sexual pleasure or happiness. Usually one partner suffers.

It is true that the Bible teaches mutual submission in the marriage relationship (1 Corinthians

7:1-5). However, insisting on your rights often alienates the one you supposedly love and damages the emotional and spiritual unity you should also be enjoying. We believe it is better to ask the following questions:

1. Is there anything I am currently doing that is offensive to you or you would rather not do?
2. Is there something you would like to do that we are not currently doing?

These are important questions. We believe that sexual pleasure is very much related to sexual understanding and unity. Marital partners should be in agreement about what takes place in the bedroom.

4. *Sexual pleasure is based on the approval of God.*

Eat, O friends! Drink, yes drink deeply,
O beloved ones!

Who is speaking in this verse? Some say that these words are spoken by the daughters of Jerusalem, who are observing the married couple on their wedding night! This we find hard to accept, because it is none of their business what Solomon and Abishag do in terms of their sexual pleasure.

We think the best view is that God is doing the speaking. If this is so, then sexual pleasure has the direct approval of God Himself.

If God is speaking in Song of Solomon 5:1b, then He invited this couple to "drink deeply." This means to be intoxicated with each other's sexual desire and passion. It matches the teaching of Proverbs 5:18-20, where the same idea of intoxication is used.

When sexual pleasure is enjoyed to its fullest, the feeling is like being intoxicated. Your mind, emotions, and responses are carried away by the drawing power of sexual passion and desire.

In marriage, a couple is simply giving to each other, and the result is edification, building each other up and strengthening each other's life.

What a beautiful relationship is pictured in these verses! Husband and wife, mutually giving to each other their respective desires and passion: no restraint . . . no reluctance . . . no inhibitions . . . no fears . . . no selfishness. Here is romantic love from God's point of view!

5

Why He's So Special

Abishag had a dream in chapter 5 that revealed the need to resolve sexual problems that arise within the marriage relationship. She asked the daughters of Jerusalem to help her find Solomon. They then questioned her as to why she wanted their help and why she thought Solomon was better than anyone else. She answered them in the last part of chapter 5 but now faced their penetrating question, "Where has he gone?" They wanted to know why they should be asked to find him. Why would he leave her in the first place?

It may be only a dream and a hypothetical situation, but it was real in the emotions of Abishag. She now describes in great detail why Solomon is so special in her heart and life. It is an important passage for all wives to understand. Your husband needs praise and encouragement from you! He needs to know how much you love him and how special he is to your heart.

Restoring the Relationship

Where has your beloved gone, O fairest among women? Where has your beloved turned aside, that we may seek him with you?

There is some question about the attitude of these ladies of the court. Their words "O fairest among women" may have been said with satire and mockery. If Solomon thinks she is the most beautiful of all women, why did he leave her? Why is she so earnestly seeking him now?

All of this started when Abishag refused to get out of bed and open her bedchamber door to her husband and lover. She now realizes her mistake. It is up to her to restore the relationship with Solomon that was strained through her reluctance to have sex with him.

Marriage can be tense at times for the dumbest reasons. The most trivial matter can become a giant barrier to our communication and our love for each other. We feel stupid when we think about our oversensitive responses, and how easy it is for us to make mountains out of molehills. But it happens.

Remembering the Commitment

If marital difficulties are going to be resolved, we must remember our commitment to each other. It is "for better or for worse," we said in our vows. We like the "better." It's tough to endure the "worse."

There were two things involved in the commitment that these two lovers made on their wedding day. One involved the responsibilities which Solomon would have as the king of Israel. Verse 2 reflects this when Abishag says:

My beloved has gone to his garden, to the beds of spices, to feed his flock in the gardens, and to gather lilies.

That's romantic language for "he's got work to do!" That's a part of marital understanding. His commitment to her did not mean that he could forsake his responsibilities as king. Affairs of state had taken him away that night she refused to respond (chapter 5). Yes, he came home pretty late, but wasn't that her understanding when they got married? Will she be jealous that he must "feed his flock"?

Secondly, she remembers that their commitment to each other involved a strong relationship that could not be shaken by the business of the court or relationships with other people in the kingdom. She adds in 6:3:

I am my beloved's, and my beloved is mine. He feeds his flock among the lilies.

Do you get a little resentful when other people take your partner's time and energies? Believe us when we tell you that this can often happen in a preacher's home! A pastor's wife often gets "leftovers" in terms of her husband's time and emotions. He shares with so many people throughout the week that it becomes difficult for him to spend quality time with his wife. He is emotionally drained when he gets home.

We decided to solve this problem in our marriage by devoting one day a week to each other. When our children were small, we got a babysitter. When they were school-aged, we took them to school on that special day, spent the hours of the day with each other, and then picked them up again after school was out. We still try to spend that one day a week together. It is crucial to our marriage commitment and communication.

Praise Instead of Criticism

The insights of this particular section of the Song of Solomon are powerful. Solomon is special to Abishag because of the way he talks to her. He praises her continually rather than criticizing her. Even under the title of "constructive criticism" much damage is done.

Mary Ann was one depressed housewife! She reflected often in private conversation with others that she could not do anything right. She downgraded herself constantly, and people found it hard to be around her. The problem? A husband who criticized her and felt that this was his duty. He was trying to improve her and change her. This is what he thought was meant by "spiritual leadership."

When her husband, Robert, was confronted by a Christian friend, he expressed great surprise. His friend told him that the problem with his wife was that he was criticizing her instead of praising her. Robert did not like the implication that he was responsible for his wife's poor self-image and severe times of depression. He argued against such an opinion for several months.

Finally, during a message on the importance of a husband praising his wife (from Proverbs 31), Robert began to see what he was doing and how it was affecting his wife. Fortunately, this man was able to change, and the result in his wife's life has been utterly amazing to behold. She is a new woman with new confidence in the Lord and in what she is able to do with the Lord's help and power.

Solomon praises his wife in a way that would cause any woman to get excited. He speaks of how she affects him. He says in 6:4 that he was affected whenever he looked at her because she was so beautiful.

O my love, you are as beautiful as Tirzah, lovely as Jerusalem.

Tirzah is mentioned in 1 Kings 16:8,15,17,23. It was known for its great natural beauty and had extensive gardens. It also had an abundant water supply. Abishag had natural beauty that reminded Solomon of one of the most beautiful cities in Israel, a place where the king would love to relax and enjoy the gorgeous surroundings.

The New International Version says "overwhelm" and the New American Standard Bible uses the word "confused." This woman really touched him emotionally just by looking at him!

Let's face it—this man is in love! Abishag has captured the heart of Solomon, and he finds her irresistible! What woman would not consider such a husband special? His praise of her (instead of criticism) attracted her greatly to him.

Romantic Reflections

I went down to the garden of nuts to see the verdure of the valley, so see whether the vine had budded and the pomegranates had bloomed. Before I was even aware, my soul had made me as the chariots of my noble people.

Verse 11 reveals that she has some anxiety about how Solomon is going to respond to her after her refusal to make love with him (in her dream). The language here is poetic, and is symbolic of one who is not sure whether Solomon's love has "budded" and "bloomed" in its response. Will he hold this against her? Will he still be romantic toward her?

Our relationships need reassurance from time to time. Tensions between husband and wife can cause insecurity, no matter how long you have been married. No one wants to be shut out and rejected.

The beautiful thing about this love story is how Abishag discovered the depth of Solomon's love and forgiveness. The New International Version in verse 12 reads, "Before I realized it, my desire set me among the royal chariots of my people." She experienced in the depths of her soul an awareness of the place she had in Solomon's heart. She was his queen, riding in the royal chariots, honored before all the people of his realm. He had no hesitation; he loved her with all his heart and was not embarrassed to let everyone know that she was his bride and lover!

Love and Desire

Return, return, O Shulamite; return, return, that we may look upon you!

Who speaks these words, urging Abishag to come back to Solomon's loving arms? Perhaps the ladies of the court are the only ones urging her to come back, but we think Solomon must also be one of the speakers, if not the principal one. The New King James Version indicates this fact when it places the title above these words "The Beloved and His Friends."

What would you see in the Shulamite?

The word "Shulamite" is the feminine form of the word "Solomon." What a wonderful encouragement it must have been to Abishag to be referred to in this way! It was like saying "You belong to me; you're a part of my life, and I'm incomplete without you!

6

I Will Give You My Love

Song of Solomon 7:11-8:4

In this lovely passage Abishag does the talking and the inviting. After all, Solomon has been describing her physical attractiveness and sexual delights. He is ready, and according to the verses just preceding this section, so is she. She's ready to celebrate with him.

The Secluded Resort

Come, my beloved, let us go forth to the field; let us lodge in the villages. Let us get up early to the vineyards; let us see if the vine has budded, whether the grape blossoms are open, and the pomegranates are in bloom. There I will give you my love.

The words "there I will give you my love" emphasize that she is looking for a romantic and secluded spot to enjoy their lovemaking.

Carole and I enjoy immensely a couple of days away. It doesn't really matter where they are as long as they are "away"! We enjoy sex at home, of course, but taking a few days off and getting away from the normal routine and duties is necessary at times. A change in environment can do wonders for a couple struggling in their sexual relationship with each other. It is so helpful in terms of communication.

When was the last time you went as a couple (without your children) to a secluded spot in order to enjoy your love? Is your marriage filled with romance these days, or could you stand a little improvement?

Planning the Relationship

Abishag is going to respond to Solomon's desires for her. She has some special plans in mind, and he is going to enjoy it immensely! This sexual relationship that she has planned for him involves four things.

1. *It involves her creativity.*

The mandrakes give off a fragrance, and at our gates are pleasant fruits, all manner, new and old.

Mandrakes were considered an aphrodisiac. The Arabs called them "the servant of love." She is indicating to Solomon that she has some surprises for him when she says "At our gates are pleasant fruits, all manner, new and old." She is going to be creative in how she responds to him, and that is enjoyable to any husband.

2. *It involves her loyalty.*

Which I have laid up for you, my beloved.

Sex without loyalty is demeaning and unfulfilling. Abishag knows better. She has saved all these surprises and sexual delights just for Solomon—no one else. That's what makes their relationship with each other so special. Wives need to express that kind of devotion to their husbands as surely as husbands need to do that for their wives. The special loyalty of a wife that gives to her husband what no other man will receive is indeed attractive to him.

3. *It involves her desirability.*

I would cause you to drink of spiced wine, of the juice of my pomegranate.

What she is saying by these words is, "You're really going to enjoy it!" Abishag has no hesitation in letting Solomon know how excited she is about making love with him, and how enjoyable he will find it to be.

This is sex from God's point of view—explicit and intimate, filled with pleasure and enjoyment. There has never been a more beautiful description nor a more complete picture of marital love.

7

Why Love Is So Powerful

Song of Solomon 8:5-14

The Bible has much to say about love. First John 4:8 tells us that "God is love." He is not merely loving, but His *essential nature* is that of love. His love gives even when there is no response (Romans 5:8; 1 John 4:19), and it is a love rooted in sacrifice (1 John 3:16). The greatest moment of expressing His love was when Jesus Christ, His only Son, died on the cross for our sins (1 John 4:9,10; John 3:16).

Husbands are to love their wives like Jesus Christ loved the church and gave Himself up for her (Ephesians 5:25-27). They are to love their wives as they love their own bodies or as they love themselves (Ephesians 5:28,33).

The closing verses of the Song of Solomon reveal four things upon which God's love is based in the marriage that operates according to divine instructions. These four essentials tell us why love is so powerful between a husband and a wife. Most of us want to experience an over-powering love relationship with our spouse, but we simply do not know where to begin. This passage gives specific help.

God's Love is Based on Sexual Contentment

Verse 4 warns against awakening love and sexual passion outside of marriage. Verse 5 indicates that Solomon awakened the sexual love of Abishag.

Who is this coming up from the wilderness, leaning upon her beloved? I awakened you under the apple tree. There your mother brought you forth; there she who bore you brought you forth.

The picture of Abishag leaning upon Solomon after their sexual encounter of the previous verses is a beautiful statement on sexual contentment. She pictures one who is relaxed and fully satisfied with what took place. God's love brings that kind of sexual satisfaction and contentment.

God's Love is Based on Strong Commitment

Set me as a seal upon your heart, as a seal upon your arm; for love is as strong as death, jealousy as cruel as the grave; its flames are flames of fire, a most vehement flame. Many waters cannot quench love, nor can the floods drown it. If a man would give for love all the wealth of his house, it would be utterly despised.

No stronger words of commitment have ever been spoken! This commitment has four basic characteristics that every married couple should carefully evaluate.

1. *It is an INTIMATE commitment.*

Possession of another person's seal means that you have free access to all that he or she possesses. The heart is the source of affections and the arm is the source of strength. Abishag is laying claim to Solomon's heart and strength. She wants to be closer to his heart than anyone else's. That is vitally important in order for a relationship to be what it should be.

Does anyone else have that place in your heart? Have you felt a stronger tie to someone other than your marital partner? If you have, your commitment to your spouse is weak and is vulnerable to temptation and future difficulties.

2. *It is an INTENSE commitment.*

When Abishag says that "love is as strong as death," these are words of strong commitment. They symbolize intensity in the relationship.

3. *It is an INDESTRUCTIBLE commitment.*

"Many waters cannot quench love, nor can the floods drown it." What wonderful words! If you have God's love, then these facts are true. If your love is something less, these thoughts may not represent the level of your commitment.

Too many of us give up too easily. Our love fades under the pressure of difficult circumstances and feelings of rejection. But God's love remains no matter what kind of floods try to drown it. The pressures will come, but God's love can withstand it all.

4. *It is an INVALUABLE commitment.*

Sex can be bought, but love must be given. Some husbands try to buy their wife's love by giving expensive material gifts. That's thoughtful, but not the way to experience God's love. God's love is built on stronger stuff than "things." It flows from the heart of God and does not give itself on the basis of the other person's performance. It is produced in our hearts by the Holy Spirit of God (Romans 5:5; Galatians 5:22), and it is not a commodity which can be bought and sold.

God's Love is Based on Personal Character

Abishag's character is demonstrated in her response to Solomon.

Solomon had a vineyard at Baal Hamon; he leased the vineyard to keepers; everyone was to bring for its fruit a thousand pieces of silver. My own vineyard is before me. You, O Solomon, may have a thousand, and those who keep its fruit two hundred.

These words have brought much confusion to Bible teachers. What is meant here by this "vineyard"?

It appears that Abishag compared the rights of Solomon to administer his own possessions and her right to her own person. Another way of putting it would be, "You've got a lot, Solomon, but I'm the best vineyard you have!"

The last words of verse 12 seem to be a request for Solomon to reward her brothers, who cared for her as she was growing up. It was customary to reward the keeper of your vineyards from the profits you received from their faithful endeavors. She is simply asking Solomon to recognize the value of what he has received in her as his bride, and to appreciate the role that her family played in making it all possible. This clearly shows what kind of person Abishag really was. She did not forget her family after she was brought to Solomon's place and made his queen. That shows character.

God's Love Is Based on Intimate Companionship

You who dwell in the gardens, the companions listen for your voice—let me hear it!

Solomon wants to hear her voice. He mentioned this before, in 2:14. He desires her companionship and longs to hear what she has to say and what she feels in her heart.

Make haste, my beloved, and be like a gazelle or a young stag on the mountains of spices.

These final words from the lips of Abishag are an invitation to celebrate their sexual and romantic love. In chapter 2 she desired to be alone with him and looked forward to the time when they could be on the mountains of Bether, which means "separation." In chapter 4 he speaks of his time with her as being like the sweetest perfume to his nostrils, an absolute delight to his heart. Now, in these final words, she refers to the "mountains of spices" a clear connection to the words of 4:10,11,14-16. Her sexuality was emphasized by these "spices" which would flow from her.

The words "Make haste, my beloved" reveal how important sexual love and romance are to any marriage. We should not be apathetic and indifferent to this need, nor slow to respond to our partner's desires. It's time to "make haste"!

Romantic Lovers The Intimate Marriage

*David and Carole
Hocking*

David and Carole Hocking strongly believe that God set the Song of Solomon aside to focus our attention on the ideal of a romantic love as He intended it to be. In spite of the many books on marriage that are available in secular as well as Christian bookstores, none of them can possibly improve on the biblical teaching found in the Song of Solomon. Here is romantic love for married couples that exceeds our greatest dreams and expectations. A book that will bring understanding, healing, love, growth, and encouragement to all who read it. Greater intimacy and sharing is possible as we follow God's beautiful picture of marriage as found in the Song of Solomon.

Harvest Pocket Books

These compact pocket books are excerpted from best-selling, full-length Harvest House books. Each booklet gives the major thrust of the complete book in an inexpensive, condensed version, designed for readers on the go. Further material on each topic can be obtained by purchasing the full-length edition.